THE LITTLE BOOK OF JEWISH WISDOM

100 QUOTES, PROVERBS, AND SAYINGS FROM THE JEWISH TRADITION.

BY ILANA TUCKER

Introduction

Do you often feel a little lost? Maybe in need of some guidance? Some encouraging words to overcome a difficult time?

It is no secret that the Jewish tradition has helped shape the world that we live in. Perhaps due to the strong sense of values and ethics that are at the core of the faith.

In this book, you will read a selection of Jewish phrases, proverbs and quotes that offer a wise outlook on life and the soul, which will help you find your way closer to inner peace and tranquillity.

There is sure to be advice for any situation within these pages, you need only flip through to find it.

*If I am
not for
myself,
who will
be for me?
And if I
am only
for
myself,
what am I?
And if not
now, when?*

Hillel

The highest form of wisdom is kindness.

The Talmud

A
righteous
man falls
down seven
times and
gets up.

King Solomon, Proverbs 24:16

People often avoid making decisions out of fear of making a mistake. Actually the failure to make decisions is one of life's biggest mistakes.

Rabbi Noah Weinberg

Say little and do much.

Jewish Proverb

I ask not for a lighter burden, but broader shoulders.

Jewish Proverb

The more schooling the more wisdom.

Jewish Proverb

You can educate a fool, but you cannot make him think.

- The Talmud

God could not be everywhere , so he created Mothers.

Jewish Proverb

*Change
what you
cannot
accept.
Accept
what you
cannot
change.*

Jewish Proverb

No one has ever become poor from giving.

Anne Frank

I felt sorry for myself because I had no shoes, until I met a man who had no feet.

Jewish Proverb

How wonderful it is that nobody need wait a single moment before starting to improve the world.

Anne Frank

Who finds a faithful friend, finds a treasure.

Jewish Saying

He that can't endure the bad, will not live to see the good.

Jewish Proverb

Pride is the mask of one's own faults.

Jewish Proverb

Do not be
wise in
words - be
wise in
deeds.

Jewish Proverb

*The work
is not
upon you
to
complete,
but
neither
are you
exempt
from
trying.*

Rabbi Tar'fon, Babylonian Talmud
(Avot 2:21)

Do not be daunted by the enormity of the world's grief. Do justly now. Love mercy now. Walk humbly now. You are not obligated to complete the work, but neither are you free to abandon it.

The Talmud

If you believe breaking is possible, believe fixing is possible.

Rabbi Nachman of Breslev

I would rather rather think of life as a good book. The further you get into it, the more it begins to come together and make sense.

Rabbi Harold Kushner

These three are the marks of a Jew — a tender heart, self-respect and charity.

Hebrew Proverb

*Look at
how a
single
candle can
both defy
and define
the
darkness.*

Anne Frank

Who is wise? He who learns from everyone.

Jewish Proverb

A little bit of light pushes away a lot of darkness.

Jewish Proverb

*Just to be
is a
blessing.
Just to
live is
holy.*

Abraham Joshua Heschel

If you wait until you find the meaning of life, will there be enough life left to live meaningfully?

The Lubavitcher Rebbe

Not to have felt pain is not to have been human.

Jewish Proverb

*Silence is
a fence
around
wisdom.*

The Talmud

He who puts up with insult invites injury.

Jewish Proverb

Your biggest enemy is yourself, so be your best friend

Jewish Proverb

No one is as deaf as the man who will not listen.

Jewish Proverb

Don't sell the sun to buy a candle.

Jewish Proverb

If you want your children to be intelligent, read them fairy tales.

Albert Einstein

Whoever is happy will make others happy too.

Anne Frank

Life is a dream for the wise, a game for the fool, a comedy for the rich, a tragedy for the poor.

Sholom Aleichem

Not by might and not by power but by my spirit.

Zechariah 4:6

A half-truth is a whole lie.

Jewish Proverb

A person wrapped up in himself makes a very small package.

Jewish Proverb

*Only a
life lived
for others
is worth
living.*

Albert Einstein

Human suffering anywhere concerns men and women everywhere

.

Elie Wiesel

There may be times when we are powerless to prevent injustice, but there must never be a time when we fail to protest.

Elie Wiesel

A person should want to live: if only out of curiosity.

Yiddish Proverbs

Be the master of your will and the slave of your conscience

.

Chasidic Proverb

The wisdom of Kabbalah doesn't tell us to decrease our egos, but how to use them correctly.

A bird that you set free may be caught again, but a word that escapes your lips will not return.

Jewish Proverb 、

*Coincidenc
e is God's
way of
staying
anonymous.*

Jewish Proverb

He that gives should not remember, he that receives should not forget.

The Talmud

Justice,
justice
you shall
pursue.

Deuteronomy 16:20

There are only two ways to live your life. One is as though nothing is a miracle. The other is as though everything is a miracle.

Albert Einstein

The only thing that is going to save mankind is if enough people live their lives for something or someone other than

themselves

.

Leon Uris

Everyone can look inside their soul and decide what they can do to make a world at peace, to end this fighting

*that goes
on every
day around
the world.*

Ruth Gruber

The
opposite
of love is
not hate,
it's
indifferen
ce. The
opposite
of art is
not
ugliness,
it's

*indifferen
ce. The
opposite
of faith
is not
heresy,
it's
indifferen
ce. And
the
opposite
of life is
not death,*

it's indifference.

Elie Wiesel

Forgivenes s is the key to action and freedom.

Hannah Arendt

*No matter
how bad
things
get,
you've got
to go on
living,
even if it
kills you.*

Sholom Aleichem

Youth is happy because it has the capacity to see beauty. Anyone who keeps the ability to see beauty

never
grows old.

Franz Kafka

Without heroes, we're all plain people and don't know how far we can go.

Bernard Malamud

Take the risk of thinking for yourself, much more happiness, truth, beauty, and wisdom will come

*to you
that way.*

Christopher Hitchens

I don't think life is absurd. I think we are all here for a huge purpose. I think we shrink from the immensity of the purpose we are here for.

Norman Mailer

If you are not a better person tomorrow than you are today, what need have you for a tomorrow?

Rebbe Nachman of Breslov

A dream which has not been interprete d is like a letter unread.

Hebrew Proverb

All dreams are fulfilled according to how they are interpreted.

The Talmud

The end result of wisdom is good deeds.

The Talmud

We don't see things the way they are. We see them the way we are.

The Talmud

For the sake of peace one may lie, but peace itself should never be a lie.

The Talmud

*Listen to
your enemy
because
God is
talking.*

Jewish Proverb

To break an oral agreement which is not legally binding is morally wrong.

The Talmud

The divine spirit does not reside in any except the joyful heart.

The Talmud

A quotation at the right moment is like bread to the famished.

The Talmud

When you add to the truth you subtract from it.

The Talmud

Anticipate charity by preventing poverty.

Maimonides

No disease that can be treated by diet should be treated by any other means.

Maimonides

Accept the truth from wherever it comes.

Maimonides

Truth does not become more true by virtue of the fact that the entire world agrees with it, nor less so even if the whole world disagrees with it.

Maimonides

When you hold a part of the essence, you hold all of it.

Baal Shem Tov

Marriage is giving it your all, and appreciating that you are but a half.

Chassidic Proverb

Certain opportunit ies are so lofty, that they cannot be accessed by the conscience self; they can only come about

*by
mistake.*

Chassidic Proverb

A
pessimist
confronted
with two
bad
choices,
chooses
both.

Jewish Proverb

*We are all
part of
each
other,
each with
our own
unique
purpose.*

Jewish Proverb

Do not be wicked in your own eyes.

Perkei Avot, Wisdom of our fathers

Everything in your life is a gift and an opportunity to heal.

Jewish Proverb

What the daughter does, the mother did.

Jewish Proverb

We are worth what we are willing to share with others.

Rabbi Jonathan Sacks

He who gives charity in secret is greater than Moses.

The Talmud

Bad habits are easier to abandon today than tomorrow.

Yiddish Proverb

Cherish criticism for it will place you on the true heights.

Rabbi Dovber of Lubavitch

A man should live if only to satisfy his curiosity.

Yiddish Proverb

Pay attention to your dreams for they are letters from God.

Jewish Proverb

In choosing a friend, go up a step.

Jewish Proverb

First mend yourself, and then mend others.

Jewish Proverb

*Life is
the
greatest
bargain —
we get it
for
nothing.*

Yiddish Proverb

When you have no choice, mobilize the spirit of courage.

Jewish Proverb

God is closest to those with broken hearts.

Jewish Proverb

A mother understands what a child does not say.

Jewish Proverb

Take care of yourself, you never know when the world will need you.

Hillel

Experience commonplac e deeds as spiritual adventures , feel the hidden love and wisdom in all things.

Abraham Joshua Heschel

A person who seeks help for a friend, while needy himself, will be answered first.

The Talmud

*Live well,
it is the
greatest
revenge.*

The Talmud

*First
learn,
then
teach.*

The Talmud

*Whatever
you find
in your
power to
do, do it!*

Kohelet (Ecclesiastes) 9:10

Made in the USA
Las Vegas, NV
02 October 2024